S0-AVA-726

# Before You Wake

*Good Dreams and Healing Thoughts*

## By Eric Kyser

*Easy Break, First Time Publishing*
*Cupertino*

© Copyright 1997 by Eric Kyser.

Photography by Ron Wenzler.
Photography on pages 36 and 42 by Thomas Fjallstam.

All rights reserved. No part of this publication may be reproduced or transmitted in any form or by any means, electronic or mechanical, including photocopy, recording, or any information storage and retrieval system, without permission in writing from the publisher.

Requests for permissions to make copies of any part of the work should be mailed to Permissions, in care of: "Before You Wake", P. O. Box 2242, Cupertino, CA 95015-2242.

ISBN: 0-9641606-7-6

Printed in the United States of America.

# *Before You Wake*

## *Good Dreams and Healing Thoughts*

Love from

E— Kyper

I have a question
    that only you
        can answer.

I seek a gift
    that only you
        can give.

I have a dream
    that only you
        can share.

I have a heart
    that only you
        can mend.

Be at peace
    this evening.
Night is for dreams,
    not worries.

Before you wake,
    things will be different.
Before the sunrise,
    hope will be near.

Ron Wenzler

Did they call your
         feelings an "obsession"?
           Typical!

What do they know
         about leasing a heart
           with no terms?

What's happened
         can't be wished away;
             only dreamed away
      for a night—
          and lessened by
              our touch.

Whose fault was it?
    I'll give you a hint:
        not yours.

"It wasn't your fault."
    In any way.

Let's accept those words
    and start healing.

I saw you today
    and felt a familiar
        helplessness.
Who am I?
    What could I hope
        to give?
What could I hope
    to make for you?

Ron Wenzler

Be still.
    Be heard.
        Be held.

Feel strength
    even as I hold
        you up.

Believe there is
    nothing to be
        sorry about.

Don't wonder 'why'
    if only for now.

Hero:

Ron Wenzler

One who gives us strength
without making us
feel weak.

I need your voice,
    calling out, comforting me;
        soothing me at night.

I need your touch—
    bringing my healing,
        caressing all my hurt.

I need your care,
    that I never stand alone;
        that I know I'm
understood.

I need your heart—
    beating close to mine.

Divide your grief.
Let me take some.

Ron Wenzler

Ron Wenzler

Make plans:
    we'll share them.

Have dreams:
    we'll live them.

Whisper secrets:
    'til you can tell me.

Bundle up. . .
    until I'm there.

Things you can do...

Repeat yourself
Sing
Stay up late
Rant 'n rave
Cry-and see if it helps
Laugh
Swing
Get on your high horse
Go on a tangent
Gallivant
Obsess
Break stuff
Make a mess
Throw a hissy fit
Throw a regular fit
Throw a terrible fit
Ask me to hold you.

Ron Wenzler

You're like a kid—
     and that's wonderful.

Kids are trusting,
     silly; creative.

Kids are always
     looking up.

In my case . . .

God heard.
     God answered.

It was man who said
     all "no's."

Heaven is where the waiting ends.

Ron Wenzler

You teach me
      everything there is
         to know
about love,
     about goodness . . .
         about you.

'Bed time' <u>tonight</u>
    is whenever you're tired.

Today is new;
        today is different . . .
        today I'm with you.

Someone to talk to,
Someone to care for me.
Someone who needs my help.
Someone . . . beautiful.

Letting me know
        I'm still blessed.
Letting me know
        I am loved.

The rest of my life
starts now . . . with you.

## 3 Things

Teach me
    and I will be wise.

Forgive me
    and I will be pure.

Love me
    and I will be
        whole.

I've never really
    belonged to anyone.

No one's ever really
    belonged to me.

I long to know the
    experience.

You fill my days
(and nights)
with compassion
and hope.
You fill my life
with beauty.

"I love you."
That's how we can begin.
That's how we'll
never end.

Childhood . . .

Ron Wenzler

When all you
wanted out of life
was a tree house,
staying up late,
your next birthday
and wings.

Ron Wenzler

Just think
    if I were there
    to look into your eyes
    when you need
    someone to listen.

Just think
    If I were there
    to hold you
    when you need
    a friend to care.

# Hiding

Light green and dark:
Shades that hid me—as a child.
Warm in the cover and still
In the leaves, hearing the sounds
Of a world far away.
Covered and safe—and blessed
To be small, I hide.
One with no rights, but free—
To be lost...
finding the strength
In contemptible weakness.

Ron Wenzler

## Overlooked

It's the poor who love
the simple gifts,
the child who delights
in the rainbow;
the meek who cherish
the notice of the special
and the sensitive who know
the touch of God.

Ron Wenzler

Come away with me
to kite-flying
hillsides,
to grass-made cots
that face the clouds.
Spend the day
and stay beside me—
helper, lover,
caring friend.

## Painter of Dreams

Streaks of silver,
Shades of blue:
Peaceful waters are painted
Before me; bringing to life
The rainbows on kindergarten
easels,
She painted a sunset each
Moment she smiled.
Mobile clouds, a name on a chair -
Joy like a half-day of school:
Like running to one who loves
When set free, such was the
Dream-painter's touch upon me.

## Stones

I wish that I was
> without sin . . .
> not so that I could cast
> the first stone,
> but to gather many stones
> into an alter of thanks.

Ron Wenzler

Destiny

There comes a point
          when you stop deciding
what you're going to be,
          and realize who you are.

# Diversity

Teachers once tried
    to get us to draw with
    a single-color crayon,
    but our hearts knew better—
    for we had already
    discovered
        rainbows.

Ron Wenzler

# The Silence of Rags

She's going through the trash again,
Looking for certain kinds of rags.
And no one knows why -
But SHE knows.
Garbage doesn't hurt your feelings.
It doesn't tell you you're fat.
Trash doesn't mind if you sing.
It's always there; it doesn't ignore you.
Trash will listen to anything—
It doesn't tell you it's heard it before.
Trash is yours to keep,
It won't reject you . . .
Rags always seem to understand.
She can't be hurt, in the silence of rags.

Ron Wenzler

When I look
at you,
I see the beauty
God created—
firsthand

Thomas Fjallstam

# In Montecito

There was a pond, where I
    used to pray; roads that
    seemed to beckon: calling to
        places, new each turn—
    moments bought, but always earned.
Blessed wonder, so little known;
    she knows we need to be alone,
    and that we need her beauty.
Ever keep your secret trails,
    your springs and lovers' shelters:
    our reclaimed Eden, free of fall—
        sight that few since Eden saw.
If they'll have you, garden stay;
    join our mornings to our play.
Let our children find your paths
    and learn in forests
        beauty lasts.

Why God Made Swings . . .

Ron Wenzler

To let the children fly,
To give a poor man
a carriage;
To humble a proud man—
and to get us used
to angel piggybacks.

With you . . .
   life invites us
       out to play.

With you . . .
   life suddenly
       became fair.

# Clay

Long have I waited,
Long will I know you:
Love you and cherish
        and call you 'my own'.
Beauty is His gift—
        and you are His artwork:
The craft of loving hands.
New loveliness finds itself
In you daily, as the Sculptor
Smoothes and recreates:
Ever young, ever beautiful;
                so, ever more. . .
Delicate woman of clay
        from the garden of above.

Ron Wenzler

Thomas Fjallstam

## Sensual

I see the gracefulness
    of your form.
I hear the gentleness
    of your voice.
I taste the riches
    of your tender kiss.
I feel the goodness
    of your precious
      soul.

Ron Wenzler

# Authority

To think I am "in charge"
of you—
that I can "order" you
to let me care.
To think I "rule above you",
that I kneel to beg
you're mine.
To imagine that I "lead" you,
so I guide you to my arms;
To realize that I "own" you. . .
just to give myself
to you.

I didn't know where to go
        and you led me.
I didn't know where to stay:
        you took me in.
I didn't know what to feel
        and you held me.
I didn't know what to say . . .
        except 'thank you.'

I think of
        the kind of life
        you  give me:
Unpredictable;
        filled with laughter—
        filled with beauty.
Always knowing a friend
        is close by . . .
        always a reason for hope.
I think of
        the kind of person
                you are:
        the rarity, the soul;
        that incredible heart.
'We' will always be.
There will always be
                the 'us.'
Our legacy is love
                itself.

# Experience

I know now compassion
for my pain is in your heart.
I know now understanding
for you have listened to my voice.
I know now of need
for I have been apart from you.
I know now of beauty:
I have seen you close
within my arms.

So this is love:
    touching every part
        of the day;
    making me
        this happy.
Caring — and doing —
    for beautiful you.

You are what healing
is all about.

Ron Wenzler

Ron Wenzler

## In Heavenly Peace

While she's sleeping, dreaming
Love, toys can come alive;
A bedroom becomes Wonderland,
Kept quiet for her sake.
This tiny, tucked-in princess;
Warring world, for once, be still.
Come soft to see her, look with joy
And leave in hope's renewal.
Sweet ballerina, taut on stand,
Breaks free for freedom's dance:
To join in watch, just close to her,
And healing, unfelt touch . . .
Light mist outside, work begins;
Unseen Master's craft:
A rainbow granted, and prepared,
While precious sister naps.

Let's think more
like kids . . .
Ones who get excited
because our tomatoes
are turning red.

We miss little things . . .
'til we kneel.

Ron Wenzler

I said,
      "What would I do
            without you?"
You replied,
      "You don't <u>have</u>
            to do without me."

Praise the Lord.

I have known peace,
joy, warmth,
comfort;
A precious healing
and a cherished
calm . . .
I have felt your hand.

Ron Wenzler

# Mom

A strange concoction
    is a Mom:
        Sheriff, drill sergeant
coach, nurse—parent

With a heart that
    shines through
        at unlikely moments

We finally see the warmth
    that was hiding all along.

We see we have a friend,
    a fan, a princess . . .

The angel, visibly protecting;
    the one juror whose vote
        is always acquittal.

She cannot be forgotten.

She is too deep in our hearts.

Advice To A Sister

Celebrate your beauty
Dare to be gentle
Give of your warmth
    and expect to be
        cherished.

Ron Wenzler

## More Things You Can Do:

Read under the covers
Pillow fight
Get too silly
Play with your food
Stay indoors
Talk to strangers
Stay home from school
Play in the mud
Not "wish you had of"
Not even wish you hadn't of
Bang shopping carts
Not finish your vegetables
Slide on the kitchen floor
   in your socks
Get on your hands 'n knees
Have cake for breakfast
See if there's a surprise
   under your bed
Have two birthdays
Hide in bushes
Zoom down hills
Pretend you can fly
Wish upon a Star
Get rocked to sleep.

## In The Marshlands


I feel close to you here,
      because it's so beautiful.
I think of you here,
      because it gives peace.
I can see you, now—
      as splendid as the sunset . . .
I hear you, beside the vast waters:
      speaking to my heart.

Ron Wenzler

Ron Wenzler

Hope
Go ahead.
Your hope is
        in God.

Dream.
Go ahead.
Your dreams are
        in His care.

The sea brings
     a place for us;
     a soft playground
     and comforting mist.
Joyous communion
     where all are taken;
     sun-filled days
     and chains are broken.

So much to cover,
So much to see:
So much to live for,
       suddenly.

Ron Wenzler

Yesterday
      has perished.
Tomorrow
      is unborn.
Today
      is life.

Thank you
    for taking my hand—
        and saying,
    as no words can,
"I'm with you."

Help me
    to put
        yesterday behind.

Help me
    to go on,
        in the presence
    of you.

Ron Wenzler

In the evening,
      in my favorite time,
           you're there.
In sorrow,
In my deepest need,
      you're found.
In my arms,
      in my longing grasp,
I'll find you there;
      you're always there.
Healing me, loving me;
Caring 'til the morning
      comes.

## Assignment For Today

You've got a whole
　　　package of dreams,
　　　　now.

So go open it.

Ron Wenzler

Ron Wenzler

If there's still a sunrise,
    there's hope.
If there's still a rainbow,
    there is still redemption.
If there's still a sunset
    there is tomorrow.

If there's you, and me . . .
    there's love.

There is still
       inspiration in your voice
     and great love within
          your touch . . .

Don't stop
touching
my heart.

Ron Wenzler

Thanks to. . .



Carol, Ciera, and Zachary Davies

Michelle, Mark and Christopher Wenzler

Celeste Ames

Priscilla Russell

Gary Wayne—who said,

"Why don't you write a poem about Montecito?"
and

Julia Haggard Kyser—who convinced me that
the world was waiting.  (Thanks, Mom.)



Gibyahkeys,


ERIC.